LIFEBLOCKERS
The Sleep Edition

The REAL Facts On How To Overcome Insomnia

Lillian Nejad, PhD

www.omnipsych.com

1st Edition

Copyright © 2018 Published by Omnipsych Pty Ltd

All Rights Reserved. No part of this publication may be reproduced, stored in a retrieval system or transmitted in any form by any means electronic, mechanical, photocopying, recording or otherwise without the prior written permission of the publishers and copyright holders.

Please direct your inquiries to info@omnipsych.com

ISBN: 978-0-6482405-2-5

Table of Contents

AUTHOR'S STATEMENT	4
INTRODUCTION	7
CHAPTER 1: The Facts About Sleep	9
CHAPTER 2: Creating a Sleep-Friendly Environment	18
CHAPTER 3: Daytime Deeds	21
CHAPTER 4: The Right Routine	23
CHAPTER 5: Sleep-Blocking Thoughts	27
CHAPTER 6: When Your Sleeping Problem is a Symptom of Something Else	30
CHAPTER 7: It's Not Working, Now What?	39
CHAPTER 8: Sleep Quiz	45
APPENDIX A: Sleep Logbook	48
APPENDIX B: Sleep Strategies Logbook	51
KEY REFERENCES	54
DISCLAIMER	55
ACKNOWLEDGMENTS	56

AUTHOR'S STATEMENT

Consider me your self-help curator providing you with REAL strategies based on REAL evidence and REAL experience.

Let's face it, there is a lot of junk out there in the realm of self-published self-help books. These days, it's hard to tell who is a real expert and who isn't, what is credible information and what isn't, what is self-help and what could actually be self-harm.

Now, I know that we are all time poor and no one has time to fact-check everything and everyone. And if someone has a website stating that they are an expert in this or that—then they must be, right?? Not right. A simple tip: if someone is an actual expert then there will be more than one website that verifies their credentials and a google search should yield dozens of links that corroborate the author's claims about their work and experience. Dozens.

So now that you know you could be easily swindled, I can let you know that I am here to help. Real help. Not fake help. Not help because I want to make a quick buck but help because I actually want to help people and have been in the business of helping people for over 20 years as a clinical psychologist. It has been my life's work to provide evidence-based psychological services and resources to clients, mental health professionals, and the general public; to promote accurate and nonjudgmental views about mental health; and to assist people to effectively address these issues with skills and strategies that work.

My full profile is available on my website: www.omnipsych.com where you can find details about my areas of expertise, links to my previous publications including, "Treating Stress and Anxiety: A Practitioner's Guide to Evidence-Based Approaches" and the CD, "Relaxation: Techniques to Reduce Anxiety and Stress and Enhance Well-being", and information about my private practice.

But as I said, you can not be sure I am who I say I am with just the 'about' section of my website. For verification, you can look me up in the official register of psychologists in Australia—where I live and work. You can also google me—there are at least 10 pages of links that verify my identity and credentials. You'll also find some unrelated stuff like I won a competition for creating a new gelato flavor, I write art, entertainment and food reviews for weekendnotes.com just for fun, and my hair color has changed considerably over the years!

Okay, so here's what I am really offering. My books will provide you with strategies and skills that work; that is, research has shown that these approaches are effective in dealing with the issue of concern. Everything that I suggest will be backed up by evidence and I can point you in the direction of the actual evidence if you want to see it for yourself. For those of you who are prepared to trust me (Not an option!! Have you been paying attention to any of this!?), but if you are, well, you're in luck, because you can.

And now comes the mission statement—To provide REAL information and strategies for a variety of psychological problems, issues and disorders based on REAL evidence and REAL experience—in an accessible, genuine and engaging manner that I hope fosters positive change for everyone involved.

Just consider me your self-help curator. But only for the stuff I know about. Because even an 'expert' doesn't know everything.

Stay tuned for more books in the LIFEBLOCKERS series.

To get the scoop, subscribe on www.lifeblockers.com.

INTRODUCTION

LIFEBLOCKERS are the obstacles that prevent you from living the life you want for yourself. LIFEBLOCKERS include emotions, thoughts, behaviors, activities and relationships that interfere with pursuing your true goals and desires.

All books in the LIFEBLOCKERS series, will help you identify, manage and overcome your LIFEBLOCKERS with effective evidence-based strategies so that you can pursue the life you really want.

LIFEBLOCKERS: The Sleep Edition is the first book in the LIFEBLOCKERS series and aims to help you address your difficulties related to insomnia.

Insomnia is the ultimate LIFEBLOCKER because getting enough sleep is absolutely necessary for your health and well-being and a prolonged lack of sleep can have a negative impact on all aspects of your life.

Each chapter in this book targets a different factor that can interfere with your sleep: the environment, what you do during the day, what you do before you go to bed, unhelpful thoughts, and other problems and disorders you may have in addition to insomnia. This book is short and to the point so my recommendation is to read Chapter 1 on the *Facts About Sleep,* and then either read all of it, or skim through all of it and then go back to the most relevant chapters.

After reading this book, you will be able to:

- identify whether you have insomnia
- use evidence-based strategies that help manage your environment, thoughts, behaviors, and emotions to improve your ability to fall asleep and stay asleep, and
- ascertain whether self-help is sufficient or whether you require specialist professional treatment to overcome insomnia.

It's time to assert yourself, ***"Insomnia—stop lifeblocking me!"***

Chapter 1: The Facts About Sleep

Sleep is one of our basic needs like food and water. It's so vital for our survival that our bodies function best when we spend a third of our life doing it!

> **Fun fact:** if you live to 81, you'll spend 27 years sleeping!

Not only do we need sleep to function, a good night's sleep has a number of health benefits, the most important of which is that we are likely to live longer and suffer less from age-related physical and cognitive decline. Conversely, the lack of sleep increases your risk for a number of mental and physical health conditions. The list of problems associated with insomnia is surprisingly extensive (see list below) and this is why this LIFEBLOCKER must be stopped!

The Long List of Ways Insomnia is a LIFEBLOCKER

A chronic lack of sleep can have a detrimental impact on your daily functioning, your emotional wellbeing and your physical health.

Daily functioning:

- Can't think clearly
- Decreases reaction time
- Perform more poorly in tasks requiring hand-eye coordination

- Affects your ability to concentrate, plan and make decisions
- Feel mentally and physically tired during the day
- Poorer work performance and productivity

Emotional Health:
- It makes you grouchy
- Increases emotional distress
- Increases anxiety
- Increases your risk for depression
- Extreme sleep deprivation can lead to psychotic symptoms
- Can trigger manic episodes in people with bipolar disorder

Physical Health (more research is needed to substantiate the following claims):
- Increases the risk of high blood pressure
- Increases the risk of heart disease
- Increases the risk of weight gain and obesity
- Increases the risk of Type 2 diabetes
- Increases your risk of injury (falls, work, driving)
- Suppresses your immune system
- Increases your risk for infections
- Can increase inflammation in your body

What happens when we sleep?

There are a number of biological mechanisms involved in sleep and going into detail about them are beyond the scope of this book, but if you are interested in the nitty gritty, the National Institute of Health has a great summary in their online article,Brain Basics: Understanding Sleep. The sections on *sleep anatomy, sleep stages, sleep mechanisms* and *the role of genes and neurotransmitters* are especially illuminating. Simply put, your body is programmed to sleep for around 8 hours every night via a number of internal mechanisms and some of these processes rely on external cues to function efficiently and effectively. If any of these internal or external factors are not present or not in sync, insomnia can ensue.

What's important: quantity or quality?

If this question is posed about sleep in general, then the answer is, of course, both are important. We need a certain amount of sleep and sleep needs to be sufficiently restorative in order for us to function well. However, in relation to insomnia, although both remain important, there is far more evidence supporting focusing your efforts on achieving the optimal quantity of sleep.

Why focus on quantity over quality? The main reasons are:
1. There is a wealth of research to support assertions made about how many hours of sleep are necessary and ideal

2. There is far less research to support claims about how to ensure sleep quality or about how sleep quality is related to the occurrence and treatment of insomnia
3. The definition of sleep quality and the way that it is measured vary widely among studies
4. Most research on sleep quality have not included participants with insomnia

So, if you come across suggestions about when or how you should sleep to improve the quality of your sleep, just know that they are probably based on emerging data rather than a solid evidence base. That doesn't mean these claims are false, just that we need more high quality studies before we can affirm that they are true. The aim of this book is to present information and strategies that are based on sufficient evidence. Therefore, in working towards overcoming insomnia, the focus will be on achieving the quantity of sleep that you need and want.

How much sleep do you need?

The amount of sleep that people need varies according to age, with newborns needing the most sleep, 14-17 hours/day, and adults age 65+ needing the least amount, 7-8 hours/day. Everyone has their own optimum number of hours they need to function at their best, but most adults need 7 to 9 hours of sleep.

You can work out your optimum sleep levels by keeping a simple sleep log: write down how many hours you have slept and rate how rested you feel when you wake up. If you feel rested and have energy, then you are sleeping enough. If you feel groggy and fatigued, then you may need more sleep.

> *If you are getting enough hours of sleep and still feel groggy, you should consult a doctor to rule out another condition like sleep apnea.*

When does a problem become a disorder?

Everybody has trouble sleeping sometimes. Sleepless nights are common when we are experiencing stress, or jetlag or even if we're really excited about something. Having an occasional night with little to no sleep will have little impact on your daily functioning, besides feeling a bit tired the next day. However, if you are part of the 10-15% of the adult population that has persistent sleeping difficulties, then you've probably noticed that it is causing problems in one or more areas of your life.

Insomnia, simply put, is difficulty falling or staying asleep. In clinical terms, difficulty falling asleep, called *sleep-onset insomnia*, is when it takes more than half an hour to fall asleep. Difficulty staying asleep, called *sleep-maintenance insomnia*, can mean that you wake several times a night or you may wake up much earlier than usual and not be able to get back to sleep. Sleep-onset insomnia is more common in early adulthood whereas sleep maintenance problems usually affect older adults and the elderly.

Certain criteria need to be met for your sleeping problem to be considered a clinical disorder. According to the latest Diagnostic Statistical Manual of Psychiatric Disorders, also known as the DSM-5, for your sleeping problem to be considered a diagnosable sleep disorder, your sleeping difficulties must occur at least 3 times a week for 3 months and cause significant distress and impairment to one or more areas of your life (social, work, relationships).

This is what you might have noticed:
- You are spending loads of time in bed not sleeping
- You feel tired when you wake up
- You feel extremely sleepy and irritable during the day,
- You often worry about how much sleep you are going to get
- You feel like you can't cope with your usual responsibilities

Sound like you? Then, insomnia is a LIFEBLOCKER whether you have a clinical disorder or not.

There are two forms of insomnia: primary and secondary—or are there…?

Until recently, insomnia was classified as a primary or secondary condition. Primary insomnia is a problem that occurs on its own and not due to or in association with another problem or disorder. Secondary insomnia refers to insomnia occurring in conjunction with another disorder or issue. Insomnia is often secondary to psychological conditions like anxiety and depression or another sleep disorder and to a range of medical conditions like chronic pain or Parkinson's disease. Insomnia can also be a side effect of using or withdrawing from a variety of medications and substances.

The removal of this distinction between primary and secondary insomnia in the DSM-5 is significant because it suggests that no matter how it begins or what condition it is associated with, insomnia requires its own evidence-based treatment alongside treatment for any co-occurring problems or disorders.

Although it is helpful to understand the possible causes of insomnia, it's not always necessary for treatment. It is more important to understand why insomnia persists and this is often due to our own thoughts, feelings, behaviors and circumstances. The strategies detailed in this book target these maintaining factors and can be successfully applied to both primary and secondary conditions.

Okay, you have insomnia, now what?

Before you read about all the helpful strategies, I'd like to tell you the best way to use this book. This is your opportunity to really understand what is going on with your sleep.

To rid yourself of this LIFEBLOCKER, you need to first identify your sleeping pattern. You will find a useful tool called the "Sleep Logbook" in Appendix A of this book to record the important information including when you go to bed, when you fall asleep, how many times you wake up and for how long, and ratings for how you feel when you wake up and during the day. You will also record what you think may have contributed to any difficulties you may have had falling or staying asleep. If it helps, you can use devices like FitBit or Up by Jawbone or the app SleepBot to help you monitor your sleeping patterns. All of this information, gathered over a couple of weeks will serve as both baseline data that you can compare to after you have used some of the strategies detailed in this book, and it will help you work out which strategies may be of most benefit to you to improve your sleep.

I recommend that you implement one or two changes at a time. Each chapter targets a different factor that can interfere with your sleep: the environment, what you do during the day, what you do before you go to bed, unhelpful thoughts, and other problems and disorders you may have in addition to insomnia. You can go straight to the chapter that you think is most relevant to you or you can read all of them and then decide which one or two strategies you would like to try first.

Once you have chosen one or two strategies, go to Appendix B to find the "Sleep Strategies Logbook" so you can track your progress. Remember, it can take a few weeks to see results. If you find you're becoming impatient or frustrated or that you are not applying the strategies consistently, don't worry, there are so many resources out there to keep you on track. This is the focus of the last chapter: when and where to get extra help! This chapter includes online resources and also details evidence-based strategies that are most effectively implemented with the assistance of a sleep specialist.

The most important thing to know is that insomnia is a LIFEBLOCKER you can overcome through strategies that are backed by years of research. Focus your energy on putting in place what you need to succeed.

You know yourself; do what you know works best for you. Now let's get to it!

Chapter 2: Creating a Sleep-Friendly Environment

The environment in your bedroom can have a significant impact on your ability to sleep. There are a number of practical ways to create a sleep-inducing environment that can be implemented easily and immediately.

Be Cool

The ideal ambient temperature can range from 63 to 68 degrees Fahrenheit (17 to 20 degrees Celsius) while temperatures above 75 degrees Fahrenheit (24 degrees Celsius) and below 55 degrees Fahrenheit (13 degrees Celsius) can cause you to wake up before you are ready.

If you do not have an air conditioner or heating, you can regulate the temperature by using fans, blinds and shades and by opening the windows.

Cozy Up

Make your bedroom feel peaceful and pleasant. Don't use the bed or bedroom for work or studying as this can create clutter and can associate the room with stress and demands rather than relaxation.

Ensure that you have a comfortable mattress and pillow that support your head and neck and invest in nice sheets and sleepwear that you look forward to slipping into every night.

Conceal Light

Light stimulates the brain to wakefulness, so you will sleep better in a completely dark room. Unfortunately, these days, we have lights beaming from every direction because of all the electronic devices we use. Charge your phones, tablets, and laptops in other rooms so the lights—as well as the temptation to use these devices—do not interfere with your sleep. Try heavy curtains or eyeshades to block out any other unwanted light. If you feel uncomfortable with total darkness, try a soft nightlight.

Control Noise

If you are frequently exposed to noise that is abrupt, unfamiliar, irregular, or intense, you are likely to have disrupted sleep. White noise can help you stay asleep despite these disturbances. Keep a fan going next to your bed to combat noise pollution or consider investing in noise-canceling headphones or noise-reducing earplugs. Of course, this is not going to be your go-to strategy if it is important for you to hear noise, like if you have a newborn. In this case, you may have to accept that your sleep will be disrupted for a while, but at least it's for a good reason!

Unconscious coupling

You may decide to go all Gwyneth Paltrow and consciously uncouple from your partner if you can't agree on the sleeping conditions that suit both of you best! You may like to fall asleep to music while your partner prefers total silence; you want the room warm and your partner wants it cool; you like to read to fall asleep, but your partner needs total darkness. And it can feel like sleeping with the enemy when your partner is contributing to your sleeping problem—snoring is a common complaint.

What's the answer? If you want to stay with your partner, then you better brush up on your negotiating skills and figure out some practical and creative ways to ensure you both sleep well.

> **Helpful hints for snoring:** *check out some anti-snoring products, go to bed before your partner so you fall asleep first, use noise-canceling headphones, or use earplugs.*

Chapter 3: Daytime Deeds

It may be what you are doing during the day that is keeping you up at night. Check out what to do and what not to do to help promote better sleeping patterns.

Catnaps are for cats

Feeling like taking a little nap during the day? You snooze, you definitely lose.

Napping interferes with the natural processes of your body clock. Naps make you feel less tired at night and associate sleeping with daytime rather than nighttime.

You are better off going to bed earlier than you are taking a nap during the day. If you absolutely can't keep your eyes open, go to bed (not the couch) and limit a nap to 20 minutes. Set an alarm on your phone or clock or ask someone to wake you up so you ensure you don't sleep longer than 20 minutes.

Over-stimulated

Stimulants contained in food, drinks and other substances interfere with sleep. Well-known stimulants like caffeine (coffee, tea, fizzy drinks) and high doses of nicotine (cigarettes) can keep you up at night. Also, be aware of a lesser known stimulant, tyrosine, found in chocolate and cheddar cheese.

Everyone's body reacts differently to various stimulants so get to know your personal limits. For instance, some people can drink coffee after dinner and still fall asleep at night; whereas others, can only have one coffee a day, but only before 2pm.

***Tip:** If you are on any prescription or over-the-counter medications, ask your doctor or pharmacist if they can lead to sleeping problems.*

Consume wisely

If you go to bed too hungry, you might be sleep-starved as well. If you're feeling famished before bed, have a light snack but avoid foods that cause gas (beans, peanuts, vegetables), that are high in fat and sugar, or that contain stimulants. And if you're using alcohol to get to sleep, stop. Alcohol may help you fall asleep, but it can lead to restless sleep and problems staying asleep.

Shiftwork

It is well established that shiftwork can lead to a variety of sleep disturbances including trouble falling asleep when you need to during the day and feeling fatigued at night when you are at work. It even has its own name, "Shift Work Sleep Disorder". If this is you, it may be time to consider other employment options... However, depending on the work that you do and your financial constraints, this is not always possible. If you plan to do shiftwork long-term, consult a sleep specialist who can give you personalized assistance based on your specific working conditions; this is likely to include a specific sleep/wake schedule and bright light treatment.

Chapter 4: The Right Routine

Having a routine can be helpful in many areas of your life, including sleep, but only if it's the right one! Is your sleep routine helping or hindering your ability to fall asleep and stay asleep? These strategies will help you stay on the right track.

Develop helpful rituals

Develop bedtime rituals that help you relax and unwind like listening to soothing music, washing your face, reading a few pages of a book, doing gentle stretches or doing a brief meditation. With daily repetition, your routine will become a cue for your body to prepare it for sleep.

Be mindful of unhelpful rituals like eating chocolate, drinking caffeinated drinks, playing online games, watching stimulating TV shows or movies, and participating in vigorous exercise within two hours of your bedtime.

Expend energy

Getting physical during the day will prepare you both physically and mentally for sleep. Regular exercise lowers your general level of stress, improves your mood and will help your body feel sufficiently fatigued by bedtime.

Avoid strenuous exercise two hours before bedtime as your body needs time to wind down. Sex, on the other hand, promotes sleep, so have at it!

Relax

If you feel stressed during the day, this can impact your sleep at night. A state of relaxation is incompatible with tension and there are a variety of ways to achieve a calm mindset before bed like gentle stretching, mindfulness and meditative practices, soothing music and relaxation exercises. Relaxation exercises, in particular, have been shown to be an effective sleeping aid but don't just stop there. Regular practice (at any time during the day) can reduce your overall levels of stress and eventually help you achieve a relaxed state more quickly and easily. And here's where I plug my CD, *"Relaxation: Techniques to Reduce Anxiety and Stress and Enhance Well-being"* available on Amazon.com. The CD is particularly useful for beginners and has a variety of exercises including progressive muscle relaxation and visualization exercises.

Progressive muscle relaxation, or PMR, developed by Dr Edmund Jacobson in 1938, involves tensing different muscles for 10 to 15 seconds and then relaxing them to create a deep state of relaxation. PMR is the most evidence-based relaxation technique for stress and anxiety reduction and has been shown to be effective in reducing insomnia and chronic pain. Visualization involves imagining a calming and peaceful place, either real (beach, top of a mountain, bubble bath) or fantasy (in a bubble, on another planet, in a fairytale).

For more relaxation exercises, see my app suggestions in Chapter 6.

Biological Bedtime

Research indicates we are born morning people or night owls so choose a bedtime that fits your biological tendency as well as your personal preferences and obligations. First, work out when you want to wake up and then count back your optimal number of hours of sleep—that's your bedtime. So if you are a night owl who needs to get up for work at 7am and you have worked out you have the most energy when you get 7.5 hours of sleep, then your optimal bedtime will be 11:30pm. If you are a morning person who likes to wake up at 5am and you need 8 hours of sleep, your bedtime will be 9pm.

Try not to vary your bedtime too much during weekends and holidays and remember to factor in your pre-sleep rituals that may take between five and twenty minutes.

Sleep when you're sleepy

A common scenario: You're sitting on the couch finding it difficult to keep your eyes open but you just *have to* finish the last 20 minutes of the movie or TV show or you *need* to read just one more chapter. So you stay up and by the time you want to go to sleep, you are wide awake! Why? There is a natural sleep-wake cycle of about sixty to ninety minutes so if you delay sleep when you are feeling sleepy you may miss your window. Bottom line: when you feel sleepy, go straight to bed!

Have an awake routine

Can't sleep? Have a routine for that too. If you can't fall asleep or you wake up and can't get back to sleep, rather than laying there stewing, develop a calming routine that will be at the very least relaxing, and at best, will help you fall back asleep.

Suggested activities include reading (nothing too exciting or stimulating), doing a relaxation exercise, listening to soothing sounds or music, or drinking warm milk or chamomile tea. Go back to bed when you start feeling sleepy and remember that lying in bed in a relaxed state is the next best thing to sleep.

Chapter 5: Sleep-Blocking Thoughts

One of the main factors that influence sleep is what you are thinking about before sleep. Beyond general worries and significant events that may keep you awake, thoughts that keep you up at night can be grouped into two categories: thinking about your sleep problem and worries about what will happen if you can't get to sleep.

Common sleep-blocking thoughts and tips on how to manage them:

"I'm never going to be able to sleep!"
Not with that attitude. Pessimism is not going to help. In fact, the belief that you will be able to sleep, or sleep self-efficacy, is linked to lower severity of insomnia and better outcomes in treatment. Replace your thought with something helpful or realistic like, "I have the information and tools I need to get to sleep," "I am doing what I can to get a better night's sleep," or "I may have trouble getting to sleep but I am likely to get fall asleep eventually."

"I am the worst sleeper!"

Labeling yourself as a loser in the sleep department is self-defeating; if you are finding replacing your thoughts with more realistic ones difficult, then you can use the mindfulness technique of just noticing when you are having the thought and then noticing that thought being replaced by another, without getting involved or attaching too much meaning to the thoughts themselves.

"I've been awake FOREVER!"

It probably feels like forever, but this is highly likely to be an exaggeration of the facts. Focus on making your environment as sleep-friendly as possible and remember that you can still benefit from resting calmly.

"I hate this!"

Fair enough. Not being able to sleep can be extremely frustrating. But working yourself up into an emotional state is counterproductive. Calm yourself down by doing breathing and relaxation exercises.

"I have to get to sleep (or else)!"

Putting yourself under pressure is the opposite of the mindset that prepares you for falling and staying asleep. Tell yourself that you can cope whether you get sleep or not. This is likely to take the pressure off, putting yourself in a better position to have a good night's sleep.

"I can't function without sleep!"

Not only can your thoughts be unhelpful, but they are often inaccurate. Remember, your thoughts are not facts. You may not be at your best with little to no sleep, but if you had an objective look at your ability to cope in the past, you will most likely find that you have been able to function to an adequate degree in at least some areas in your life. If you can dispute this thought effectively, then you are likely to feel less anxious and stressed about the next day's work/home/life demands. And if you're less stressed, you might even be able to get some sleep!

In some cases, this thought may be accurate. If so, you won't solve your problems by worrying about them at night. Prepare for this during the day by planning what you will do if you are not able function well enough to complete your usual responsibilities. Being prepared for this possibility will reduce your worries about it at night, and put you in a better position to fall asleep.

One last tip:

It's clear that negative pre-sleep cognitions can have a negative impact on sleep; but what about positive thoughts? Turns out gratitude is related to positive sleeping patterns including decreased time to fall asleep, better sleep quality and duration, and less daytime dysfunction. Not only will a daily focus on gratitude improve your sleep, research shows that a grateful mindset can also increase happiness, life satisfaction and resilience, improve overall health, and reduce anxiety and depression.

So you can add—**start a gratitude journal** to your pre-sleep routine. It is as simple as writing down three new things that you are grateful for every night. In the space of only a few weeks, you'll find that your mind becomes more naturally attuned to the positive aspects of your life making you more resilient to sleep-blocking thoughts and also giving you the best chance to have a good night's sleep.

Think well, sleep well.

Chapter 6: When Your Sleeping Problem is a Symptom of Something Else

It is far more common for insomnia to be associated with another problem than it is for it to occur on its own. Insomnia occurring without the presence of another disorder or problem (medical, psychological, substance use), represents only a small proportion, 10%, of insomnia sufferers. So, if you're among the 10-15% of the population that struggles with insomnia, it is more likely that something else is also going on. Also, given that insomnia is a risk factor for developing other problems, it's important to know what they are and what to do if they are affecting you. The most commonly associated problems are described below. If you think you might be experiencing any of these issues, consult a health professional as soon as possible.

Depression

Trouble sleeping is one of the symptoms of Depression and to make matters confusing, sleeping problems can also lead people to become depressed. It's the old chicken or the egg conundrum. Changes in sleeping patterns for individuals with clinical depression include trouble falling asleep but the most common issue is waking up too early and not being able to get back to sleep.

Other symptoms of clinical depression include: changes in appetite, low energy, fatigue, low motivation, low mood, not enjoying things you used to enjoy, withdrawal from others, feelings of guilt and hopelessness, and thoughts of worthlessness and suicide. If you are experiencing these symptoms, see your GP or a mental health professional like a psychiatrist or clinical psychologist who can assess your symptoms, and recommend the appropriate treatment which should include psychological therapy and possibly anti-depressant medication.

If you have suicidal thoughts, even for only one day, seek assistance immediately to ensure your safety and to receive the appropriate support.

Anxiety and Stress

Anxiety is often characterized by excessive worry and is one of the main culprits interfering with our sleep. When worry leads to problems sleeping, you feel fatigued during the day, which makes you feel less capable of dealing with life's demands resulting in even higher levels of anxiety and stress. Then you can add being concerned about falling asleep to your list of worries which just makes it less likely that you will ever get a good night's sleep! Learn to break the stress–sleep cycle by using the following strategies.

Lose sleep over it

You can expect to lose sleep under certain circumstances, like when you have a big exam, presentation or interview the next day; when you are planning your wedding; when you have a newborn and when you are dealing with difficult times in your life due to illness or loss. During these times, the best thing to do is accept that you will probably lose sleep.

Accepting the reality of your situation takes the pressure off trying to get to sleep and may make your feel more relaxed. And it's worth noting, if you are able to lie in bed in a relaxed state, it can be almost as restorative as sleeping all night.

Contain your brain

Worrying is a common occurrence, and part of our normal daily (and often nightly) thought processes. Bedtime is the most inconvenient time to worry for you, but not for your brain. There are no distractions, you are not multi-tasking, so suddenly our brain says, "Hmmm, it's nice and quiet, seems like a good time to worry!" To keep your brain in check, satisfy its need to worry during the day—when and where it suits you most.

Use the following three strategies together to contain your brain:

- *Worry place*—Decide where is the best place for you to worry. It should be somewhere you have access to everyday, most likely a room in your house, but not your bedroom. Once you decide where your worry place is, this is the only place you allow yourself to spend significant time to process your worries.
- *Worry time*—Set aside a particular time of day to worry. Be specific e.g. 10-11am.

Discipline yourself to worry only during your worry time in your worry place.

- **Worry container**— Use this strategy to help you contain your worries to your time and place. Clearly, you are going to have worry thoughts pop in your head at all times of the day and night so here is what you do. Carry notecards or post-its and a pen with you and whenever you have a worry, write it down and put it in a container (if you're out, this may be your wallet or handbag and if you're at home, you may have a specific worry box or jar that you can put your notecards into). Make sure to keep some notecards and a pen near your bed, for worries that take place before sleep.

By writing down your worry and putting it in a box (or jar or bag), you are literally containing it until your designated worry time. This means your brain can be rest assured (pun intended) that you will attend to this worry when it is appropriate. During your worry time, in your worry place, you can read your worries from your container. You may find that by the time you read them, they are no longer worth worrying about! But if they are, use your worry time effectively by focusing on solutions.

These suggestions may seem silly, but if worrying is a major obstacle for you, they are worth a try.

Sound asleep

Worry is counter to the state of relaxation you need to fall asleep. Listening to soothing sounds and relaxation exercises before bed can help refocus your mind on calming thoughts and images and help you release tension. Progressive muscle relaxation and autogenic relaxation exercises are two kinds are relaxation exercises that can be useful in aiding sleep. You can find these and other useful techniques in the following apps:

- **Relax Melodies**: Calming sounds to help you sleep
- **Relax and Sleep Well**: Hypnosis and meditation recordings
- **Sleep Pillow Sounds**: Provides ambient, white noise sounds to help you sleep
- **Calm**: Apple 'Best of 2018' app with meditation and sleep stories
- **Insight Timer:** Sleep section with music, stories & relaxation exercises including one by me called "Progressive Muscle Relaxation for Sleep."

These apps have been selected because they satisfy three criteria: they are available on both iOS and Android devices, they have a rating of at least 4 (out of 5) by users, and they are low-cost, free or have a free version.

Substance Use

The effects of alcohol, caffeine and nicotine on sleep have been discussed (see Chapter on Daytime Deeds) but there is another substance that can be detrimental to getting your sleeping back on track—sleeping pills. Sleeping pills are part of a class of prescription medication called benzodiazepines, the most common being Valium.

These medications can be helpful for short-term sleeping problems that may occur due to specific stressors like the death of a loved one, a stressful incident or severe jet lag. But for longer term insomnia, sleeping medications do not address the factors that are causing or maintaining the problem.

Furthermore, the recommended maximum duration of use for this class of drugs is two weeks. Unfortunately, many people take them for much longer than that which can lead to increased tolerance and dependence. Continued use will also interfere with strategies that you implement to train your body to adopt a healthier sleeping pattern.

If you have been prescribed a benzodiazepine by your treating doctor, make sure that you are taking them as prescribed. If you want to reduce or cease your use of this medication, only do so under the supervision of your treating doctor or psychiatrist. It is not recommended to cease long-term use suddenly or by yourself as you may experience severe withdrawal effects.

Due to the problems associated with benzodiazepines, a new class of sleeping pills known as non-benzodiazepine hypnotics or new generation hypnotics are now more commonly recommended and prescribed for insomnia. So far, these medications have shown moderate effects in improving sleep onset and maintenance with minimal side effects. However, they have not been sufficiently tested with all cohorts like the elderly, people with certain medical conditions and people with substance abuse issues. Ensure that you consult your doctor before taking any prescription medication for insomnia.

In addition to prescription medication, illicit substances particularly speed, cocaine and other stimulants are also detrimental to sleep functioning. If you are using any medications or substances, it is important to disclose this to your treating doctor so they can fully assess the impact of these substances on your problems sleeping. You may need to consider treatment for substance use or dependence as a pathway to improving your sleep.

Another Sleep Disorder

Sleep apnea

Sleep apnea is a sleep disorder involving interrupted breathing (usually for 10 seconds to one minute) until the person wakes up in their effort to breathe again.

This disorder often affects older adults, particularly those who have gained weight and lost muscle tone. Loud snoring, feeling groggy when you wake up, and feeling tired during the day are common symptoms of sleep apnea. If you suspect that sleep apnea is disrupting your sleep, speak with a health professional immediately, as this can be a life-threatening issue. Also be sure that you do not take any sedative medications or substances before sleep as this may prevent you from waking to resume breathing.

Nightmares

Everyone knows what it feels like to have a bad dream and it's normal to have a nightmare now and then. However, some people may experience severe disruptions to their sleep due to recurrent and vivid nightmares. There are ways to alter the impact of your nightmares by writing them down and then re-scripting them (often with an alternative pleasing ending) and then rehearsing your new version while you are awake.

This process both exposes you to the nightmare making it less scary and anxiety-provoking and it prepares your mind to modify the nightmare when you're sleeping so they don't cause distress and wake you up. Nightmares can be associated with a history of trauma and is a common symptom of post-traumatic stress disorder. If this is the case for you, consult a mental health professional who specializes in trauma to assist you with this and other associated symptoms of trauma.

A Medical/Physical Condition

Sleeping problems often co-exist with other medical and physical problems and illnesses including pregnancy, chronic pain, Alzheimer's disease, Parkinson's disease, cancer, heart disease, stroke and head injuries. Insomnia may be a byproduct of physical discomfort caused by the condition, due to the brain changes associated with the condition and/or a side effect of medications taken to treat the condition.

Consult a health professional to ascertain the causes of your insomnia and ensure that appropriate attention is given to treat insomnia alongside your medical or physical issues.

Chapter 7: It's not working, now what?

So you tried everything and you still can't sleep.

For optimum success, the sleep strategies need to be implemented systematically and consistently and this requires a great deal of organization, discipline and patience. So understandably, it can be difficult to apply these changes on your own.

You may feel unmotivated or find it difficult to be consistent or you may feel frustrated by the whole process and how long it is taking. Because there are a number of emotional, cognitive, behavioral, physiological and situational factors that can affect your sleep, you would be forgiven for feeling overwhelmed and for not knowing where to start.

It might be time to ask for help!

Sleep specialists can guide you with additional strategies that may include psychological treatment (CBT-I), specific regimens like sleep restriction therapy (SRT), and pharmaceutical sleeping aids like melatonin that are best employed under professional supervision.

Cognitive-Behavioral Therapy for Insomnia (CBT-I)

CBT-I is a six to twelve-week psychological treatment protocol specifically for treating insomnia and is recommended as the first-line treatment for insomnia by the National Institute of Health, The American

Academy of Sleep Medicine and the British Association of Psychopharmacology.

Multiple studies have shown that CBT-I improves both the quantity and the quality of sleep. CBT-I includes many of the strategies that have been outlined in this book but spends more time on helping you identify and modify unhelpful thoughts and beliefs that are impacting on your sleep and your ability to function well during the day. The benefit of seeing a mental health professional who specializes in sleeping problems is that he or she can personalize your program based on your specific difficulties and individual circumstances. However, there are a number of online programs based on the CBT-I protocol that may be of benefit, ranging from a 5 week program to a 12 month program if you think you may benefit from longer-term support.

- **CBT-I Conquering Insomnia Program** www.cbtforinsomnia.com: 5 week cognitive behavioral treatment basic program is USD 44.95
- **SHUT-I** www.myshuti.com: 26 week self-help program is USD 149.00
- **Sleepio** www.sleepio.com: 12 month program is USD 400.00

Sleep Restriction Therapy (SRT)

SRT is a component of CBT-I treatment for insomnia that aims to correct circadian rhythm dysfunction by retraining your body to be sleepy at the appropriate time. In other words, it's pushing the reset button on your body clock. If you have been taking benzodiazepine medication, you must cease this (under the supervision of your doctor) before you commence this treatment.

Sleep restriction starts by limiting the time you spend in bed, so it would be more aptly named 'bed restriction therapy'! The first step is to record the time you spend sleeping every night for a couple of weeks so you can ascertain your average duration of sleep. Make sure to record your bedtime, the times you woke up during sleep, the time you spent asleep, and the time you got up on a daily basis (see the Sleep Logbook in Appendix A). The idea is to only spend this many hours in bed. So, if you spend about 8 hours in bed every night but only 5 of those hours sleeping, then the treatment would begin by restricting your time in bed to only 5 hours a night (the minimum sleep restriction time is four hours).

You then set the time you go to bed based on the time you need to wake up. If you want to wake up at 7am, and you are only allowed to spend 5 hours in bed, then your bedtime would be 2am. Importantly, you must wake up at your designated time and you are not to take naps during the day.

Every night your sleep efficiency is calculated (total sleep time/time spent in bed x 100) and when your sleep efficiency reaches 90% (80% if you are age 65+), your time in bed is increased by 15 minutes at a time. This process continues until you reach your ideal sleep time or core sleep requirement. Everyone has different sleep requirements but the minimum is considered 5 hours per night while most need between 7 to 9 hours and some need up to 10 hours. Your sleep specialist can assist you with ascertaining your core sleep requirement.

There are some side effects with SRT, particularly in the beginning of treatment—mainly feeling tired during the day and some people experience headaches. To assist with regulating your sleep, your sleep specialist may recommend bright light treatment (sitting in front of a special light box that emits fluorescent light) to use during the day. As you may not be functioning at your best during the initial stages of treatment, ensure you are not overexerting yourself during the day or operating heavy machinery.

SRT requires a lot of patience and discipline. A sleep specialist can personalize your treatment and help keep you on track. Research has shown that this is an effective treatment with long-lasting benefits including being able to fall asleep earlier, having a more consistent sleeping pattern and having better sleep quality. Expect to see significant changes to your sleeping pattern after a month of treatment.

Example of SRT Process

Step 1: My Sleep Logbook over two weeks shows that, on average, I spend 5 hours sleeping out of 8 hours in bed. I need to wake up at 7am to get to work on time, so I set my bedtime at 2am

Step 2: I go to bed at 2am and wake up at 7am no matter how sleepy I am at night or in the morning.

Step 3: I calculate my sleep efficiency every night and increase time in bed by 15 minutes if sleep efficiency is 90% or more.

> **Night 1:** went to bed at 2am, fell asleep at 2:30, woke up at 4:30am, went back to sleep at 5 am and woke up at 7 am.
>
> Total sleep time = 4 hours
>
> Time spent in bed = 5 hours
>
> Calculation 4/5 x 100 = 80%--no change to protocol
>
> **Night 2:** went to bed at 2am, fell asleep at 2:15, woke up at 7 am.
>
> Calculation 4.75/5 x 100 = 95%
>
> If Sleep Efficiency is over 90%--can increase time spent in bed by 15 minutes
>
> **Night 3:** went to bed at 1:45 am, fell asleep at 2am, woke up at 7 am
>
> Sleep Efficiency: 95%--can increase time spent in bed by 15 minutes
>
> **Night 4:** went to bed at 1:30 am ...

Step 4: This process continues until I reach my core requirement of sleep

Melatonin

Melatonin is a naturally occurring hormone in your body that is involved in your sleep/wake cycle. This hormone is affected by the time of day and exposure to light, increasing at night to assist with sleep onset and decreasing at sunrise to elicit wakefulness.

Melatonin production declines as you age which may account for some of the sleeping difficulties encountered by older adults and the elderly. Synthetic melatonin is now available as an over-the-counter dietary supplement but proceed with caution! Melatonin should only be taken under the care and supervision of your doctor or sleep specialist as it has side effects, can interfere with other medications you are taking, may contain a higher dose of melatonin than is needed, and can be counterproductive if taken at the wrong time of day. Also, the evidence supporting the use of melatonin for insomnia is modest at best. Some studies show that melatonin may help with symptoms associated with insomnia while other studies show no benefit at all.

Other commonly suggested sleeping aids that you ingest include chamomile tea, valerian, magnesium, and homeopathic formulas and supplements that contain a variety of ingredients. So far, there is no conclusive evidence for the use of any of these herbal remedies either alone or in combination.

Many more rigorous studies are needed before melatonin or any other supplement can be considered effective and safe for long-term use. If you are taking or thinking about taking any supplements, make sure you tell your doctor what you are taking to ensure your safety and to help maximize their effectiveness in your overall plan to improve your sleep.

Chapter 8: Sleep Quiz

Let's see how much you know after reading this book! Read the following questions and circle the correct answer.

1. How much sleep do you need?
    A. About 7.5 hours a night
    B. Between 5 and 10 hours
    C. It depends on the individual—if you feel rested and you don't feel tired all the time, you're probably getting enough sleep.
    D. All of the above

Answer: D. Everyone has their own optimum number of hours, with most adults having a core requirement of 7 to 9 hours a night. The important thing to note is how you feel when you wake up and during the day. If you feel rested and have energy, then you are sleeping enough. If you feel groggy and fatigued, then you may need more sleep.

2. What is Insomnia?
    A. Not being able to fall asleep
    B. Waking up very early in the morning and not being able to go back to sleep
    C. Having difficulty staying asleep during the night
    D. All of the above plus feeling tired during the day

Answer: D. Insomnia can present in several different ways and is considered a problem when it is prolonged and it interferes with your life when you are awake.

3. What behaviors can interfere with my ability to sleep during the night?

      A. Napping during the day
      B. Eating cheese
      C. Watching a scary movie
      D. All of the above

Answer D. Yes, the answer is always going to be D! Sometimes we don't know what we're doing to contribute to our problems; the good news is you will find out what to do and what not to do to improve your sleep.

4. Sleeping well depends on:

      A. Your sleeping environment
      B. Your pre-sleep routine
      C. Your behaviors during the day
      D. Your levels of stress and anxiety
      E. All of the above

Answer E. Okay, so the answer is E this time, but you get the picture. Sleeping well depends on several factors but you may need to focus on only one area or even one strategy to make significant improvements in your sleep. Start by targeting one area that you think is affecting your sleep the most and then choose one or two strategies to focus on and assess the results.

If you have had long-term sleeping problems, it may take several weeks to get your sleep back on track so don't lose hope.

APPENDIX A: Sleep Logbook

If you want to improve your sleep, one of the most important steps is to identify your current sleeping patterns. You can use a diary or a logbook to record pertinent information about your sleep (see the sample logbook provided).

The information you need to record includes the following:

- Date
- Time you went to bed
- Time you fell asleep
- Number of times you woke up during the night and how long you were awake each time
- Time you woke up in the morning
- Total hours you spent in bed
- Total hours of sleep
- How you felt when you woke up—refreshed or tired
- The level of fatigue during the day rating it from 1 (not at all) to 10 (extremely)
- Anything that might have affected your sleep that night

Sample entry:

- *Date: 12/10/17*
- *Went to bed at 10:30pm*
- *Fell asleep at 11:30*
- *Woke up twice during the night, 1st time 12:15am for 15 min and 2nd time 3am for 30 min*

- Time I woke up in the morning 7am
- Total hours spent in bed 8.5 hours
- Total hours of sleep 6.75 hours
- Felt tired when woke up
- Fatigue during day 7/10
- What may have affected my sleep: drank a glass of wine before bed, had to get up to go to the bathroom

Recording this information over a period of one to two weeks will help you identify your current sleeping patterns, clarify how your sleeping patterns are affecting you during the day, and discover what may be contributing to the problems you are having falling and/or staying asleep.

If you decide to seek professional help, this information will be extremely helpful and will assist the clinician to choose the best treatment for you.

You can record this information on a chart like the sample logbook provided.

To download a printable copy of this logbook, go to www.omnipsych.com/resources.

LIFEBLOCKERS: The Sleep Edition

Date	Time went to bed	Time fell asleep	# of times woke up and how long awake	Time woke up	Total hours in bed	Total hours of sleep	Did you wake up Refreshed or Tired?	Rate level of Fatigue during the day from 1 (not at all) to 10 (extremely)	Write down anything that might have affected your sleep last night.
12/10	10:30pm	11:30pm	2 times 1st 15 min 2nd 30 min	7am	8.5 hrs	6.75 hrs	Tired	7/10	Drank glass of wine before bed, had to get up to pee

To download a printable copy of this logbook, go to www.omnipsych.com/resources.

APPENDIX B: Sleep Strategies Logbook

When you are trying to improve your sleep, it is important to keep track of what strategies you are using and rate their effectiveness over time with respect to your specific goals. Your goals may include one or more of the following: to fall asleep more quickly, to have less disrupted sleep, to sleep longer or to feel less tired during the day.

You can use a diary or a logbook to record pertinent information (see the sample logbook provided).

The information you need to record includes the following:
- Date
- Strategies you are using
- Time it took for you to fall asleep
- Total hours of sleep
- The level of fatigue during the day rating it from 1 (not at all) to 10 (extremely)

Sample entry:
- *Date: 24/10/17*
- *Strategies: Dark room, relaxation exercise*
- *Took 15 minutes to fall asleep*
- *Woke up one time*
- *Total hours of sleep 6.5 hours*
- *Fatigue during day 5/10*

Feel free to add more categories but make sure they are directly related to your goals. Record this information everyday. Start with one or two strategies so you can determine what has been useful, and remember, it can take several weeks before you see improvement in your sleep.

You can record this information on a chart like the sample logbook provided.

To download a printable copy of this logbook, go to www.omnipsych.com/resources.

Lillian Nejad, PhD

Date	Strategies Used	Time it took to fall asleep	Number of times awake	Total hours of sleep	Rate Tiredness during the day from 1 (not at all) to 10 (extremely)
24/10	Dark room Relaxation exercise	15 min	1	6.5	5/10

To download a printable copy of this logbook, go to www.omnipsych.com/resources.

KEY REFERENCES

American Psychiatric Association (2013) *Diagnostic and Statistical Manual of Mental Disorders* (5th ed.). Arlington, VA: American Psychiatric Publishing.

Edinger, J. D. & Carney C. E. (2008). Overcoming Insomnia Therapist Guide: A Cognitive-Behavioral Therapy Approach (Treatments That Work). Oxford University Press.

Hall, M. H., Smagula, S. F., Boudreau, R. M. et al. (2015). Association between Sleep Duration and Mortality Is Mediated by Markers of Inflammation and Health in Older Adults: The Health, Aging and Body Composition Study Sleep, Volume 38, Issue 2, 189–195, https://doi.org/10.5665/sleep.4394

Harvey, A. G., Stinson, K., Whitaker, K. L., Moskovitz, D., & Virk, H. (2008). The Subjective Meaning of Sleep Quality: A Comparison of Individuals with and without Insomnia. Sleep, 31 (3), 383–393.

Hirshkowitz, M., Whiton, K., Albert, S. M., et al. (2015). National Sleep Foundation's sleep time duration recommendations: methodology and results summary. Sleep Health, http://dx.doi.org/10.1016/j.sleh.2014.12.010

Sleep Disorders: In Depth (2014). https://nccih.nih.gov/health/sleep/ataglance.htm

Spielman A.J., Saskin P., & Thorpy M.J. (1987). Treatment of chronic insomnia by restriction of time in bed. Sleep, 10, 45-56.

DISCLAIMER

Any information made available in this publication (electronic or hard copy formats) and on omnipsych.com is not intended to be a substitute for professional medical advice, diagnosis, or treatment.

Readers should seek the advice of a qualified health provider with any questions regarding a potential or actual medical or psychological condition. Readers should not disregard professional medical advice or delay in seeking it at any time, including because of the content of this book or of Omnipsych.com.

If you are experiencing low mood and/or suicidal thoughts or self-harm behavior, seek professional help immediately.

The author has based this content on either current knowledge in research evidence and/or best practice guidelines. Any recommendations she has made related to other resources (websites, books, self-help programs) is purely based on her research, and she is not responsible for the content and claims of those resources.

ACKNOWLEDGMENTS

Thank you to my family and friends for your support and encouragement throughout the process of conceiving and writing the LIFEBLOCKERS series of books. Special mention goes to my husband, George, for your practical advice (even when I hated it) and for backing my passion for writing. Without your time, patience and support, this would have been impossible to achieve. Thank you to my children, Persia and Costa, for being a constant source of inspiration and joy.

Thank you to Yvette Gindidis for helping me come up with the title, LIFEBLOCKERS. You've always had a way with words! Thank you to Simone Gindidis, for the contagious energy, enthusiasm and professionalism you bring to the field of psychology. I look forward to many exciting collaborations in the future.

I must thank my wonderful friends and colleagues, Dr. Robyn Gallucci, Dr. Kylie Thomson and Ray Zylstra for volunteering your time to help me make this book a reality. It gave me peace of mind to receive positive and practical feedback from such esteemed professionals and valued friends.

Thank you to Simon Hartshorne, from PeoplePerHour, for formatting my book and designing the front and back cover. I greatly appreciated your professional guidance and your willingness to go above and beyond to get LIFEBLOCKERS ready for publication.

Thank you to Barbara Macciolli who supported my writing and was the first to publish my LIFEBLOCKERS articles. Thank you also to Zahrina Robertson for my professional headshot and planting the seed that gave me the idea to publish a series of books rather than one giant book that would have taken me another year to finish. This is far more satisfying!

To all of you who are reading LIFEBLOCKERS, I hope that this book achieves its objective to help you overcome insomnia so that you can be your best self and pursue the life that you really want.

I would love to hear from you so please leave a review and remember to subscribe to get updates on www.omnipsych.com.

Coming soon: *LIFEBLOCKERS: The Anxiety Edition.*

www.ingramcontent.com/pod-product-compliance
Lightning Source LLC
Chambersburg PA
CBHW072114290426
44110CB00014B/1909